THE EVIDENCE OF
THINGS NOT SEEN

THE EVIDENCE OF THINGS NOT SEEN

POEMS ON
THE COMMON MAN, FRIENDS,
FAITH, AND FAMILY

W. TYSON THOMPSON

TNSB
MONTGOMERY

TNSB
105 S. Court Street
Montgomery, AL 36104

ISBN 978-1-961938-03-8

The photograph on the cover is by assalve via istockphoto.com.

Printed in the United States of America.

To my family and friends,
about whom many of these poems were written.

Contents

POEMS OF FAITH

POEMS OF FAMILY

Foreword

This book was started after retirement to fill my spare time, with no thoughts of publishing. However, as the number of poems grew, and I started writing about my family, the thought occurred that they and others mentioned might like a copy. Also, I have included information about my family in which, sooner or later, the next three or four generations may be interested. For these reasons, I have decided to have the poems printed. They were a joy to write, and I hope they will bring similar joy to all who read them.

Poems for the Common Man

This seetion consists of several poems, each consisting of couplets, about common, everyday events. Some were written while I was experiencing the activity.

At the Doctor's Office

At the Doctor's office, you first must sign in.
They ask for all sort of information and then
You take a seat and you wait for the call.
You wait, wishing you were at the mall.

After waiting, you finally hear your name.
They take your weight, then ask why you came.
They take your blood pressure and temperature,
And the wait begins again, of that you can be sure.

And after the nurse, the doctor comes in.
And after small talk, the examination begins.
You are asked to sit or maybe lie down,
And tapping your stomach, he listens to the sound.

He asks questions and taps and probes,
He looks in your ears, throat, and your nose.
You are asked to cough while he uses his stethoscope.
He reads your chart and smiles, this gives you hope.

He writes a prescription, which is just another pill,
Pronounces you healthy and hands you the bill.
On the way out you are asked to pay.
The lady takes your money and says, "Have a nice day."

THE DENTIST

Going to the dentist is quite a treat.
I have a hygienist that can't be beat.
She cleans my teeth and uses the floss
And makes them white with a shiny gloss.

She will pick and scrub until they are clean
And removed all the plaque she has seen.
When all is done and she is through,
She tells you when your next visit is due.

You go to the window, there to check out.
As you leave, "I got clean teeth," you shout.
Another six months before I come back,
Unless I have trouble with my food —pack.

My New Car

A Buick LeSabre, that's my new car.
My Crown Victoria was just not up to par.
The inside is gray but the outside is white
And the seats adjust until they fit you just right.

Everything is automatic — the headlights, too.
I understand that's standard if the car is new.
The headlights come on when you put it in gear
But if the door isn't closed a buzz you will hear.

It has a compass, a radio and a clock,
And in gear, the doors automatically lock.
It has plush carpet, leather seats and a heater.
It's wide with good leg room; it's a four seater.

Which ever you need, either kilometers or miles,
You can find on the speedometer and other dials.
For safety there is something called the Onstar.
It tracks you and can tell them exactly where you arc.

If you have an accident and you can't brake
And you hit something and the airbags inflate,
They can send you emergency aid if you cannot speak,
With no worry of finding you and that's pretty neat.

It's the newest car I've ever had, a two thousand one.
I might have gotten taken but now that it's done,
I am glad I've got it. It rides and drives good
But then it's a new car and well it should.

I like my new car though it cost too much,
With automatic windows, seats and such.
But I plan to keep it for quite a long time.
I'll be glad when it's paid for and is really mine.

My Computer

The click of a switch, the tap of a key,
And the world opens up to me.
I go to Yahoo, a stock to find
To buy or sell or anything I've in mind.

Find your favorite or try something strange,
Or read your mail if your mind you change.
E-mail is easy and it is quick,
And is sent faster than a stamp you can lick.

The note you type, then click to send,
Away it goes to be read by a friend.
Some e-mail is serious, some funny,
And some will guarantee you a lot of money.

Information on your portfolio can be found.
Are you making money or losing ground?
On the Internet you can buy or sell,
If you can get in before the bell.

In genealogy, you can find the family tree.
Did you come from preachers, crooks, or royalty?
Was Grandpa Irish, English, or Portuguese,
Maybe French, or maybe none of these.

When you finish, the "start" button is found,
From there you move the cursor to "shut down."
With a whirring sound the screen goes blank,
For all of this we have technology to thank.

That Certain Room

Here I sit in that room called the "Can,"
Where everything you need is close at hand.
Where behind closed doors you can do as you please.
What you do here, dogs do to trees.

If any one saw me, it would make me blush,
So when I finish, I reach back and flush.
Sometime I write and sometime I read,
But when I leave, I've done my deed.

You can sit, you can stand, but you will lean
To wash your hands; you want them clean.
You dry with a towel, or maybe with hot air.
You want your hands dry — how, you don't care.

When you leave you feel relieved
For in a short time, fulfillment you've received.
When you finish and you are all through,
Going out the door, no one asks, "What did you do?"

On the way in, you walk fast as in the cold.
When you leave it is a leisurely stroll.
By the way you walk and the smile on your face,
It is easy to see that you appreciate this place.

It's Tax Time Again

I volunteered two days a week from February 1 until
April 16, 2001, as a tax consultant for the lower
income and elderly, which was sponsored by the AARP
in conjunction with the IRS. It was a learning and
rewarding experience and one I enjoyed.

It's tax time again . . . it's that time of year.
People get more hectic as April 15 draws near.
Why not get started early, don't wait;
By holding off, you don't get a better rate.

It just prolongs the agony, the hurt, and the pain
And by waiting 'til later, you have nothing to gain.
Get all your receipts, empty those files,
Then stack them in those neat little piles.

Get those records together, those 1099s and W2s,
Resign yourself to the fact you are going to lose.
Add capitol gains, interest and dividends,
Forget trying to keep some, there is no way to win.

Total your cost for medicine, add to this your doctor bills.
These will lower your taxes; it makes you glad you were ill.
Don't forget contributions to the church and boy scouts.
Avoid trouble; leave them off if there are any doubts.

Total all state and personal property taxes paid.
These can help you keep more of that money you made.
Interest on a home mortgage, this you can deduct.
Don't forget a dime; it will all help save a buck.

Add the IRAs and annuities, that's quite a bit of dough,
With what's left you wonder, "Where did it all go?"
I buy food and clothing and a piece of candy or two,
And when the money runs out, I just have to make do.

You know you have to pay it, you know it's true.
To have to write the check, it's just hard to do.
Write it, stamp and seal it and let it go,
Just remember the old saying, "Easy come, easy go."

Painters

I have several friends, who love to paint,
Others would like to but say they can't.
Everyone can but they may not be good,
But if they would like to, try they should.

A scene around the house, country, or seashore,
Or clouds, or trees, or fog on the moor.
As long as you can imagine it, any scene will do.
Don't worry about others as long as it pleases you.

Some paint portraits or animals, and some houses,
There is one who even paints scenes on blouses.
They say it relieves tension, eases stress,
Clears the mind and lets you rest.

It is easier to paint when there is more than one,
You need encouragement until the picture is done.
It seems if you skip a week and don't paint any,
It is harder to start back, excuses are plenty.

I have thought of painting, but have not begun.
It will take time but I think it would be fun.
One thing to consider is the time it would take —
Then there is the expense — if an artist I would make.

These things must be considered and taken into thought
Before any paints, brushes or other materials are bought.
Oh well, I will think about that another time.
I will just continue writing and save my dime.

But if to be a painter is your dream,
Take up the brush, your leisure to redeem.
Mix up the colors and begin to paint
And never entertain the notion that you can't.

A Small Town Called Opp

Opp, Alabama is a very small town.
It has the best people to be found.
They are friendly, hospitable and warm.
Into that good place, I was born.

There was one stadium with one high school.
In the summer, we gathered around the pool.
There was only one park, not many places to play.
Not all those athletic fields you find today.

You can play baseball, basketball, football or even soccer.
There are gyms with a variety of equipment, even lockers.
You have different ages playing different games,
With teams called animals, colors, and all sorts of names.

In town the stores are still open, not closed like some,
Proving if the service is good people will come.
It's service with a smile as they put it in the sack.
As you go out the door, it's a friendly, "Y'all come back!"

Everyone knows your family, they know your kin,
They'll stick by you through thick and thin.
They are pleased with your business with no traffic jam.
Aren't you glad you came from a small town, I know I am.

Where I Live

Ferndale Court is the name of my street,
A close knit neighborhood that's hard to beat.
It's so peaceful, like a walk in the park,
And so quiet and serene, even after dark.

At end of the circle is where I reside,
Behind closed curtains, for privacy, I abide.
This is where I work, I read, eat, and sleep,
Where I live and all my treasures I keep.

Three bedrooms, two baths is room enough for me,
Here I live by myself, happy as can be,
Or so I tell myself when I am sad,
Which is not often, it's a very pleasant pad.

In the back is a big yard and many fruit trees.
To rid the weeds, I spend a lot of time on my knees.
I need the exercise and the fresh air,
The sunshine with vitamin D, I get it there.

Fertilizing and watering, spring and summer, too,
I prune, trim, and spray until the fruit is due.
Doves are cooing, birds are singing in the trees,
Fruit blossoms are opening and beckoning to the bees.

The yard is a source of enjoyment and fun,
But I like it better when the work is done.
The roses are beautiful but the vines come with thorns,
In trimming the vines — my shirts — they are torn.

The trees in front are mostly Pine,
With needles so thick, grass is hard to find.
The sap from the trees fall on the ground,
Step in it and to your shoe it is bound.

Inside, winter is warm, summer is cool.
I keep it very comfortable as a rule.
It is lived in and seems somewhat in disarray
But joy and peace may be found there any day.

My Exercise Experience

When I go to work out I am a little shy,
My skinny legs and pot belly, that's why.
But Monday, Wednesday, and Friday I am there.
I get through with a groan and a prayer.

All those machines with all those weights,
They keep you healthy, they invigorate.
It causes the blood to flow, increases circulation,
To keep it up, takes real dedication.

I don't use the treadmill; I walk in my neighborhood,
But when it's cold and rainy, I probably should.
There is tennis, swimming and handball, too.
To exercise and workout, there is no lack of things to do.

To exercise my legs, I use the leg press,
It's the one I dislike the most, I must confess.
I strengthen my thighs, then exercise my back.
The doctor says it's weak, of muscles there is a lack.

After thighs and back, I work my abs next.
Then I go down stairs to build up my pecs.
To exercise my arms, I push, pull and lift.
You have to work to get these muscles; it's no gift.

Paper or Plastic

Today, I go to the grocery store
To buy bread, meat and something more.
Maybe some fruit, jelly, or jam,
Some sandwich meat or sliced ham.

I always get Fritos and TV dinners.
Campbell soups are always winners,
Orange juice and decaffeinated tea;
It doesn't take much; it's just for me.

With milk, cookies, and crackers
I head for the checkout and sackers.
I'm ready for the question as they ask it,
"Which do you prefer, paper or plastic?"

THE ONLY CHILD

To be an only child must not be too bad.
I have friends who are and they seem to have had
A full and happy life with many friends.
The saying is, "As the wind blows, so the twig bends."

Being surrounded by brothers is not what matters.
It's not the pitchers who hit the ball, it's the batters.
Standing over the plate he is alone,
But the instructions he had will get him home.

Parents are the first instructors of this lone one.
There is no instance where the influence is none.
The final person is the result of each human contact.
The changes that occur, you can't give back.

If the only child is lonely, he must share the blame,
For with disadvantages, advantages also came.
Resources were not divided, parents' love not shared.
The only child who doesn't try to succeed has erred.

The family size doesn't insure that one will succeed,
The key is to be taught the skills one will need
In order to express one self and relate to other men
So that their friendship and influence one may win.

Now that I have said all this, you may not agree.
There is one thing I failed to make known, you see
All this I just surmise, for an only child, I am not,
But three brothers and one sister, I've got.

Bring Back the Front Porch

Remember the front porch with the rocking chairs
Where we would sit and talk and share our cares,
Where the neighbors would come and sit for a talk
And say, "How y'all?," to others on their evening walk.

Many of our problems we solved sitting there
And anything we had we learned to share.
We would get along better if we had porches today
Where we could sit and hear what people had to say.

Porches would make the world a better place today,
Where we could meet and talk and have our say.
It would be great to have a rocking chair and swing
Where one could sit and listen to the birds sing.

But with the houses today, porches are few,
Especially if your house is relatively new.
Today they are no porches just a cement slab
With no place for chairs on which to sit and gab.

Let's bring back the porch and the good old days
Of solving problems, the good old simple way.
Take time to live, learn to talk again.
Take care of your neighbor, your fellowman.

Bring back the porch and the simple way of life,
Bring back the good times get rid of the strife.
Bring back the good days, a much simpler time,
But that will take more than this simple rhyme.

I'M GETTING OLDER

It's my birthday and I'm still here,
A year older, but I'll not shed a tear.
I'll spend it with those I hold dear,
In fact I think I will stand and cheer.

I am over sixty, that wonderful age
When activity slows and memory fades.
I just want to spend time in the shade.
In the book of life it's just another page.

There is no timetable, no schedule to keep.
No hurry to clean; tomorrow I'll sweep.
There is no subject, nor topic too deep,
As the mind sharpens, the body sleeps.

To keep this body, it's weight I must fight,
Anything to keep from going on a diet.
Eat reasonably, make the meal light,
And never eat a lot late at night.

At this age I love to give advice
But sometimes I have to give it twice.
If I do, I'll make it worth the price
But I'm old, I don't have to be nice.

Another birthday has come and gone —
A little less muscle, a little less brawn;
It's the same for others, I am not alone.
We reap the fruit of the seeds we've sown.

So let's help each other across the street
And maybe the traffic light we can beat.
We may be old but we can still compete
If the night is long and the game is sleep.

POEMS FOR FRIENDS

The poems in this section were written about friends and different activities involving those friends.

Christmas Light Tour, December 19, 2000

It was the week before Christmas when we went for a ride.
There was Bobo and Johnnie Ruth and Sue by my side.
We had met at Sue's for cider and to exchange gifts.
We do this every year to give our spirits a lift.

Our first stop was Chappie's for a bite to eat,
Hamburgers and fries, a combination that's hard to beat.
After finishing our food, we raced back to the car.
With the heat on high, we were warm before very far.

We rode out to Wynlakes to see the Christmas lights,
Through the subdivision where decorations were a sight.
With Wynlakes toured, we set out for The Timbers,
A place that always looks good, especially in December.

We saw the twelve days of Christmas and many other scenes,
Including several nativities, all with their own three kings.
The night was getting late and lights were being shut down.
We headed toward home, which was all across town.

With shouts of "Thanks for the presents," we went different
    ways,
With memories of the Christmas tour to last us for many days.

CHRISTMAS EVE AT BOBO'S

On Christmas Eve at Bobo's, we meet
To share fun and fellowship, and also to eat.
He will have hot soup and several desserts.
After eating, we all agree, on food he's the expert.
To sit around and talk and reminisce is great,
We enjoy the warmth and company until quite late.
Then full and happy, we scatter to the wind,
To meet the next day with family and other friends.
For Christmas is never over as long as joy is to be found,
And in our case, Christmas lasts the whole year 'round.

CHRISTMAS AT THE HALBROOKS'

Christmas at the Halbrooks' is something to behold.
For all the food and fun, I don't mind the cold.
Though it may be cold and rainy on the outside,
There is always love and warmth where we abide.

There are gifts so prettily wrapped and decorated with bows.
They are given out and exchanged with many a ho ho ho.
Did he really want a puppy or would a cat have been better?
How do you find out what she asked for in that Santa's letter?

Something for the house or something for the car,
Nothing exotic and nothing from afar,
Just a box of candy or fine stationery, will do.
We will all be grateful and hopefully, so will you.

Will the shirt be big enough, will the sweater fit?
Will the tie be worn; will the book be a hit?
It really doesn't matter. The gifts are not the reason
We again celebrate a wonderful Christmas season.

It's the love that is shared with family and friends
And just being together at the Halbrooks' once again.

Part of the Family

Family becomes more important the older you get.
The love of each person is felt more deeply and yet
There is no need to say it as often as before,
For love and caring greet you at every door.

There are smiles and laughter and hugs all around,
For warmth and joy and genuine friendships there abound.
For family consists not only of children, father, and mother,
But dear friends, with whom you can share, one with another.

Families share holidays and other important events.
They will laugh at stories whether or not they make sense.
To be family you don't have to be on the family tree,
Or have the same coat of arms of ancestry.

No, you just have to love and be loved and show that you care
And you will be part of the family and welcomed there.

FRIENDS

Good Friends know you and like you still,
They stick by you when no one else will.
They share your joy, your grief, your pain,
Help you when you're in need again and again.

You can be silent; there is no need for talk.
Sometimes it's nice just to go for a walk.
When in need, you receive without having to ask,
They are always there to help you with any task.

With them you can travel, you can go places,
And whatever you do there's a smile on their faces.
They don't condemn, ridicule or make fun of you;
They are still your friends, no matter what you do.

The thing you need from a friend you can borrow,
And don't worry if it's not returned on the morrow.
Keep it 'til whatever you are doing you have finished,
And never fear, the friendship will not be diminished.

You are not looking for gain when you lend to a friend,
And no matter the cost you would do it again.
A friend will bring presents when it's not your birthday;
Just because they want to, it's just their way.

You don't only love your friends, them you also like;
And they are still your friends whether wrong or right.
With them you can sit and talk and be at ease,
After being with a friend, it's always different when they leave.

Greathouse Family Reunion, April 22, 2001

We meet at Point A Lodge in late April or early May.
It began, as a celebration of Aunt Georgia's birthday.
It's the Greathouse reunion, the gathering of the clan,
They come from near and far, from all across the land.

It use to be for two days, now it is only one,
But all would agree, better this than none.
Some have not seen each other since last year
And everyone you see is glad that you are here.

Don't be embarrassed if you forget a name;
The situation for many others will be the same.
When you arrive there are hugs all around.
This family has the friendliest people to be found.

Some gather before lunch to catch up on the news
And to figure out just which child is whose.
They come in all sizes, both large and small,
And you will also find both short and tall.

We all look forward to getting together
And — more times than not — we have good weather.
You can walk on the dock or along the shore
And, in good weather, you couldn't ask for more.

Some throw frisbees while others play ball,
With a lot of things to do, it is your call.
Some sit and talk, stories and jokes are told.
We discuss cars, and stocks, bought and sold.

My first cousins I know and can recognize,
Past that generation and for names I have to improvise.
Whose child is this, whose husband, or whose wife is she?
You are embarrassed when told, "they are part of my family."

The love of this family is shown by hugs and smiles.
Nothing is more precious than the hug of a little child.
So many names, I'll never remember them all.
I will be doing well if half of them I recall.

We love getting together, we enjoy the crowd,
With everyone talking, it can get pretty loud.
Some will eat on the outside tables under the pines,
Others inside, planning to go back two or three times.

A long table is filled with vegetables and meats,
Also with drinks, desserts and a lot of other treats.
There is plenty of food, there is plenty to eat,
With all of these good cooks, the food can't be beat.

With ice tea in one hand, in the other, a full plate,
Eat and enjoy, forget about gaining weight.
Not long after dinner folks will begin to leave,
Bowls, cake plates and utensils, they begin to retrieve.

When good-byes are said to those you hold dear,
You leave, hoping to see them again next year.
But love is strong and next year we will return
To greet the family and a few new names to learn.

Home and Friends

Turn the heat up, get this place warm.
It's so good to be inside, out of the storm.
The thermostat is on eighty, but that's all right.
It's going to be cold and below freezing tonight.

To have a warm and dry house is a great blessing
From the ant and squirrel we can learn a lesson.
Stock up with food like the squirrel does with nuts.
This you will need, no ifs, ands, or buts.

Prepare for winter, the cold, sleet and rain,
Or you may not be around to enjoy the summer again.
The summer when everything is green and alive,
The flowers buzzing with bees from the hive.

Birds nesting, baby squirrels playing in the trees.
Fruit trees waiting for those pollinators, the bees.
Trees and bees together, each one doing a good turn.
Pay attention for there is a lesson here to learn.

Do your good deeds and be helpful to others,
That is everyone you meet and not just your brother.
For with food and shelter, there is one thing you lack,
Someone to hold and hug and who will hug you back.

Life can be full if you have all of these,
But it can be empty if you have no one to please.
So find that someone, that person, that friend,
And hold them close so you'll never be alone again.

IRENE AND BILL

The street is Ferndale Court in the northern part of town,
On the quietest little cul de sac anywhere to be found.
Nestled at the end of the circle, and in the front, pine trees,
And in the back there's always the humming of the bees.

Irene and Bill had roses, azaleas, and fruit trees, too.
We swapped seeds and plants if we ever got anything new.
I gave them a persimmon tree, she gave me a muscadine vine,
And in the summer and fall, we swapped fruit, all the time.

They were the best of neighbors and they are hard to find.
It was Irene, Bill and Lady, a family one of a kind.
They took in my paper and mail while I was away,
And for all they did for me they would never take pay.

I would cover their turbines and uncover them in the spring.
We both fed the birds, squirrels and other living things.
We had bird baths and threw out seeds and bread,
And even in the winter we made sure they were fed.

Irene and Bill lived next door for over twenty years;
With Bill gone, Irene is leaving too, or so it appears.
She is going to Louisiana to live with Frank and Heidi.
I trust she will be happy, for I will miss her mightily.

Good Neighbors

Good neighbors are hard to find,
Whether in front, beside, or behind.
When you need them, they are always there.
When you are gone to, they know not where.

They take care of your house and take in your mail
And see that no damage is done by rain, sleet, or hail.
We meet and laugh and talk across the fence,
And help each other out with no talk of recompense.

As two neighbors, Irene and Bill have been the best.
As for me, I'm afraid I've rather been a pest,
Asking them to keep an eye on things when I'm away.
When I was working, that happened for many a day.

They were always friendly with a word of cheer.
That's good because our houses are so near.
When I worked in my yard, I would edge their drive,
And by their fence, they would cut the grass on my side.

In the winter, I would cover their turbines;
They would hold the ladder while I covered mine.
Good bargains they would share with me:
A tap light in my closet to help me see.

I play with Lady who now is blind,
And when I leave, she feels left behind.
She has diabetes and sometimes is ill.
I think she is sad and still misses Bill.

We all miss Bill now that he is gone,
But think of him in his heavenly home.
We exchanged gifts and Christmas cards, too.
I am thankful for good neighbors, aren't you?

Good neighbors are truly hard to find,
Whether in front, beside, or behind.
Yes, good neighbors are hard to find,
And I am sure there are none better than mine.

Ralph Douglas Halbrooks' Birthday

*Plans had been made to celebrate Doug's birthday
and I read this at the birthday dinner.*

Doug is a dog doctor, a vet.
He works with animals and yet,
Even with people he is good
And would help them if he could.

Doug is the son of Ralph and Mary Jo, one of three
With the entire family being dose friends to me.
But Doug was the first, being in my class at school
Where in chemistry he did quite well, as a rule.

He graduated from Auburn and received his degree.
It took a lot of studying and did not come free.
Besides personal sacrifice, it took time and money
But after that, he ended up in the land of milk and honey.

Well, maybe not milk and honey, but his practice is thriving,
And you can tell from his success that he is striving
To make a difference in the lives of people and their pets
And all this because he is one of the best vets yet.

He has been successful in his chosen occupation.
It took a lot of work, a lot of time and dedication.
Success comes to those who strive to fulfill a dream.
Each mighty river begins as a trickle of a small stream.

He lives in the big house on an old plantation site
With enough land to deer hunt, much to everyone's delight.
Now a pond has been built and stocked with fish.
He seems to have everything for which one could wish.

He doctors large and small, from horses to cats
And if someone brought one in, he would even doctor bats.
To hear him talk he spends most of his time with cattle,
And I hear, those old steers can put up quite a battle.

To Dr. Ralph Douglas Halbrooks, I just want to say,
It's a pleasure to celebrate with you this forty-fifth birthday.
To such a great person and an even better vet,
I can truly say, "It was a great day when we met."

I have enjoyed the friendship, the laughter, the fun
And will cherish the time spent together when day is done.
For friends grow more precious as time goes by
And I am sure we will be friends until the day we die.

Johnnie Ruth Parker's Birthday, April 29, 2001

Johnnie Ruth, Bobo, Sue and I get together often. I wrote this poem and read it while we were out for dinner for this occasion

To Johnnie Ruth Parker, I lift my glass.
It's another birthday, another year has past.
You have grown more mellow, you have matured,
Or maybe I should say, you have endured.

You have reached retirement, that age of bliss;
You have the time, there is nothing you should miss.
A trip to the northeast, or a trip to the west,
Go wherever you please, choose whichever is best.

You can go shopping, buy a pair of shoes,
Or a gift for a friend or anything you choose.
Just stay home and rest or read a good book.
To find something to do, you don't have far to look.

To top it all off your livelihood is made.
You can sit home and do nothing and still get paid.
Retirement is great, you would have to agree,
But don't waste it all by just watching TV.

With you and your friends, we gather to celebrate,
For it's a day and occasion that just wouldn't wait.
Yes, it's another birthday, another year is gone,
But with friends such as these, you are never alone.

The Wesley Wanderers
in Cajun Country

I have made several trips with the Wesley Wanderers
from First United Methodist Church of Montgomery.
Elizabeth Cheshire works with Sr. Adult Ministries and,
along with a very active committee, plans the trips. The
trips ranged from a day trip to a week or more. These
were just two of the many trips I took with them.

The Wesley Wanderers were gathering,
happy as a lark,
It was March 19th and we were to leave
at 8 o'clock sharp.
We had to make Lafayette, Louisiana
before stopping for the night.
Traveling through the rain we made few stops,
our schedule was tight.

We did stop at Hardee's in Selma
for a bite to cat,
Everyone knows those biscuits
are hard to beat.
Through Demopolis, Meridian and on
to Hattiesburg for lunch
And back on the bus,
we were a full and happy bunch.

McDonald's in Covington, Louisiana
was our next stop,
Where Martha visited with the Maxey's,
her Mom and Pop.
In Lafayette, it was TGI Friday's
for an early dinner.
Whoever made this choice
certainly picked a winner.

The service seemed slow,
it left a lot to be desired;
Could it be those five waitresses
that were never hired?
The chef seemed to be at case,
there was no hurry.
As time to load the bus approached,
we began to worry.

Some got up and left,
there were at least two.
I won't mention any names
but one was Sue.
It took Elizabeth's authoritative voice
to get the food.
She takes care of us like a mother hen
with her brood.

"To insure promptness"
is the meaning of "tip" to many.
In this case it fit — we didn't get any
and we didn't leave any.

With jokes and laughter about it all,
I guess you could say,
It was a good time to end
a near perfect first day.

With our patience having been
put to the test,
We headed back to the motel
to get some rest.
Tuesday morning brought sunshine
and a very full day.
Beverly Lane, the local guide,
led us all the way.

She was very knowledgeable
about St. John's Cathedral and Oak Tree,
Which turned out to be
the vice president of the Live Oak Society.
After hearing the organ and
touring the adjoining cemetery,
We were behind schedule so off to Acadian village
with no time to tarry.

While some bought parched peanuts,
souvenirs or a shirt,
Others visited museums, houses
and even the church.
We had lunch at Bailey's;
the bread pudding was extra good
And I ate too much or
at least more than I should.

After lunch we passed University of Louisiana
at Lafayette's Cypress Lake.
The bus was warm and we were full,
it was hard to stay awake.
But we pushed on with Beverly's stories and
history of the land
And came to St. Martinville
with its two man Cajun band.

We toured the cathedral with its baptistery,
which was unique.
The very ornate Stations of the Cross
made one feel humble and meek.
Heard the story of Evangeline, saw the statue and
visited the Evangeline Oak,
And listened to the Romeo Brothers,
the two man band of which I spoke.

Off we go to Avery Island,
composed of a hill over a salt dome.
That's where they grow red hot peppers and
is the McIlhennys' home.
We saw the video, toured the plant and
got our sample of Tabasco Sauce,
And on the way back heard legends
of the origin of Spanish moss.

The red Tabasco sauce is hot,
as everybody knows.
The green sauce is mild,
for this they just use jalapenos.

Next, we headed to Jefferson Island
and Joseph Jefferson's home,
Which, as you guessed it,
is also located over a salt dome.

We toured the house with its antiques and
saw a beautiful peacock.
Then we saw the chimney in the lake and
the ruins of the boat dock.
The story of the drained lake was hard to believe.
We all agreed
It happened though and must have been
an unusual sight, indeed.

After saying goodbye to Beverly,
we went to Prejeans for dinner.
Now whoever picked this one,
really did pick a winner.
We had the chicken and sausage gumbo,
a good and hot dish.
Some played it safe and had chicken,
others ate alligator or crawfish.

I don't know about the crawfish,
but the alligator tasted like chicken fingers.
We were entertained by the Cajun Five Band
with the French-speaking singer.
The dessert was bread pudding
with a delicious Jack Daniel sauce
And on the way home, thank goodness,
no more stories of Spanish moss.

Then to close a near perfect day,
it was back to the Hampton Inn.
As much as we ate and as good as it was,
it surely must have been a sin.
Wednesday it was a swamp cruise
with Cajun Man and Gatorbait, his dog,
Where we saw alligators, cormorants, and
turtles sunning on a log.

He identified plants such as the Little Yellow Flower and
the source of NutraSweet.
Leaving there, we headed to the Bayou Delight
for a bite to eat.
Another treat was seeing great grand daughter,
Brittany and family.
It wasn't hard to see the Maxey's
were as proud as could be.

The drive to Baton Rouge was smooth and
gave us time to sleep,
But we had to rush to the Capitol
for an appointment we had to keep.
We saw the observation deck and
where Huey P. Long was shot,
Saw the legislative chambers
but had to leave at 4:30 on the dot.

A short rest, then on to Ralph and Kacoos
for a great dinner,
With the Mahi Mahi and pecan sweet potato pie,
it was another winner.
As for the meal and service,
I rated it among the best.
Sara's son and wife,
and June's granddaughter and friend were our guests.

Thursday morning, Hoyt and Sara were surprised
by granddaughter Mae,
Which was a very nice way
to start off the last day.
Then it was on the road again
and homeward bound,
With one site left on the schedule
before true contentment is found.

Across from sandy beaches in Biloxi is Beauvoir,
Jefferson Davis' home.
We saw the movie, toured the home and
before long, our time was gone.
With Jefferson Davis' home behind us and
the road to home ahead,
"Thank you Elizabeth for a wonderful trip,"
is the only thing left to be said.

Petals from the Past with the Wesley Wanderers, April 17, 2001

We are off again, we are on the run,
Ready for a good time, ready for fun.
It's the Wesley wanderers to Petals from the Past
To keep this group entertained is no big task.

We all gather early and load on the vans,
With Elizabeth along, we are in good hands.
Up the interstate and off to Jemison we go
Where roses from grandmother's garden still grow.

The sun is shining but the wind is cold.
On the hill, it blows often, so we are told.
In the rose garden, the wind is unyielding.
We change plans and enter the education building.

We see slides and have the lecture on roses.
It is interesting and educational, no one dozes.
Jason is knowledgeable and gives good information.
He tells of his schooling and where he got his education.

Off to the Antique Mall we go for a bite to eat.
The food is good, the apple cobbler a real treat.
A few minutes to browse, make a purchase or two;
It's an antique mall, don't expect anything new.

Back on the bus, to 'the Petals' we return
To purchase roses, lilies and maybe a fern.
We visit the gardens, then on to the gift shop,
Make a group picture and on the bus we hop.

Back to Montgomery and home with our plants
To put in our gardens, our lawns to enhance.
Another successful trip the Wesley Wanderers have completed.
Thanks to Elizabeth, without whom it would not have
    succeeded.

Mother's Day at the Lake

It was Mother's Day and I was late —
I'm so glad they decided to wait.
It was a beautiful day and a lovely drive.
A little after one and we arrived.

At last Johnnie Ruth had invited me,
It was Ben and Voncile's lake place, you see.
A place I had heard of and wanted to go.
And I'm glad she also invited Bobo.

We met the host and the rest of the crowd,
Grandchildren of whom you could be proud,
Son and daughter with spouses were there,
All were interesting with stories to share.

Ben was busy cooking on the grill.
It was delicious, I can taste it still:
Venison tenderloin on which to munch
Just a starter before a gourmet lunch.

After eating the salad, beans and such,
To get full and satisfied didn't take much.
The barbecued chicken was very good.
I had plenty, probably more than I should.

For dessert there were brownies and apple pie
And strawberry shortcake which I had to try.
Your choice of drinks from colas to iced tea.
Now this was a meal that just suited me.

It was a beautiful wooded, lake-front lot,
An ideal place when the weather gets hot.
From the screened-in porch, a beautiful view
Where a glorious sunset is always new.

Thanks for inviting us, we had a good time.
Now for the last couplet to end this little rhyme.
Relive the joy, remember the day
When we were all together in the middle of May.

Opp High School Class Reunion of '55

The graduating class of '55 of Opp High School
Had their 46-year reunion and as a rule
A good time was had by all.
With teachers, students and a principal it was well attended
Which meant, with one or two being long winded,
It was slow going through the roll call.

Mr. Sullivan was first to recall the good times past.
He was there only a short time, he couldn't last,
Before he escaped to the mill.
Mr. Merrill, the chemistry and physics teacher was next;
From his many positions and experiences he took his text.
His fondness for the class seemed real.

Dr. Lubker, Miss Bobbie Boyd, the English teacher was there.
She had come from Chapel Hill in North Carolina where
She teaches pathology of speech.
Mrs. Benton, who as a teacher was Miss Mignon Bates,
Had gray hair but still appeared to be in great shape,
Better than students she did teach.

Miss Boyd told of the influence Opp had on her.
He wouldn't read, she didn't know what his problems were.
He just wouldn't read.
He had a speech impediment and was embarrassed.
She was sensitive to him and became a teacher he cherished.
That planted the seed.

Now she is a speech pathologist, a very good one I am sure.
If it had not been for Opp, she might never have felt the lure
Of that vocation.
This means we all have profited from her tenure here
And to many more people she has also become dear,
Because of her inclination.

Richard was master of ceremonies with Harold and Taylor;
It had to be efficient with no room for failure.
Harold's invocation we did receive.
The class flower, gladiolus, green and yellow, looked real neat;
by the planning committee, the decorations were hard to beat.
The class motto: Not merely to exist but to achieve.

The reunion was a great success, a good time was had by all.
I don't know about everyone else, but I had a ball.
To Betty Parker, we do give thanks
For taking the initiative to get a brick for each person's name,
Who took chances with the money, from her account it came
When she saw Valera at the Bank.

Don't forget your friends, let's keep in touch.
As we grow older, friends mean so much,
And friendships continue to grow.
We never know what influence we have on others
Whether they are strangers or a close brother,
The seeds of kindness, may we continue to sow.

Poems of Faith

This section includes poems on faith, church, and related topics.

Faith

"Now Faith is the substance of things hoped for,
The evidence of things not seen." — Hebrews 11:1

By the word of God, worlds were framed;
From invisible things, visible things came.
Abel offered a fuller sacrifice than Cain,
A verdict of a just man from God he did obtain.

Enoch did not see death but was taken away,
Because he pleased God, for to sin he would not sway.
Noah was warned of things not seen and was bold —
He prepared an ark and saved his household.

Abraham left home and went to a foreign land,
Because of God's call, it was not Abraham's plan.
Sarah gave birth to a son when she was old
From whom came a nation, as was foretold.

Following God's word, Abraham offered up his son,
In so doing God's favor he won.
Rahab perished not with those who did not believe,
For with peace the Israelite spies, she did receive.

Moses gave up the riches of Pharaoh's palace
And chose the affliction of his people and the king's malice.
But not fearing the wrath of the King and man
Kept the Passover and crossed the Red Sea on dry land.

Upon the mighty Jericho, the Israelites did gaze,
Whose walls fell after being encircled for seven days.
No time to tell of Gideon, Barak, Samson, and others
Who in trusting God saved a nation and their brothers.

It was through faith all of the above was done
And it is through faith the heart of God is won.
Through faith all things are possible.

LOVE

Many words have been written about love,
Mainly, that which came down from above.
For that love was pure and given to all
Who would accept it and listen to its call.
The call to care for and serve your fellowman,
To feed the hungry, lift up the fallen, do what you can,
Visit the sick, care for the elderly, clothe the poor,
Do all of these and more, and you can be sure
That you will be blessed with happiness and joy,
For pure love came to earth in the form of a baby boy.

I have added my writings to those about love,
And have spoken of that which came down from above.
I trust this pure love has been accepted by all,
And that we have listened and received its call.
The call to care for and serve our fellowman,
To feed the hungry, lift up the fallen, do what we can.
Let us visit the sick, care for the elderly, clothe the poor.
When we do all of these and more, I am sure
That the many blessings of happiness and joy
Will be ours, because of that little baby boy.

Feelings of Love

There it is, this pain in my heart.
It comes most often when we part.
When we are together, all seems right
And does, until you are out of sight.

What is the meaning of this, this feeling?
I hear the music as it comes pealing,
The pealing of joy and sounds from above,
This feeling — it must be the feeling of love.

I think of you when you are not around,
Solace and peace are not to be found.
I wait for you, up and down I pace;
You appear and my heart begins to race.

The pain is gone, gone from my heart.
With joy, we are together again, never to part.
We embrace and greet each other with a kiss
And are lost once more in heavenly bliss.

Should, Would, Could

Should I or Shouldn't I?
Would I or Wouldn't I?
Could I or Couldn't I?

These must be answered in every situation,
For every circumstance and every contemplation.
And if, for the first one, the answer is no,
The others do not matter; that's as far as we must go.
If the answer to the first question is yes,
Then we must continue and give it our best.

The second question, "Would I?" is an important one.
It is what the end result will depend upon.
If I would, and it needs to be done,
And we do not, we must have a good reason.
Then it may be that I would not.
If this be the case, it is better to be forgot.

Then the third one we must think about.
It is one we must consider and figure out.
If the answer is no, then why waste time trying,
You try hard but cannot, and end up crying.
But if the answer is yes, get up and get going,
You'll never have a garden without the sowing.

Sunday and Church

It is Sunday morning, the first day of the week.
Get out of bed, take a shower, get a bite to eat.
I must get ready; today I go to Sunday school
Where I study the scriptures and the golden rule.

Ridgecrest Baptist Church is the one I attend,
Where you can always count on meeting a friend.
In Sunday school, we study the Bible, God's holy word
And listen to the sweetest music you have ever heard.

The fellowship and love for each other are evident
And the Spirit of God is forever a resident.
We sing praise choruses and some of the old hymns
Of Christ and His love and His royal diadem.

To find a more Christ-like staff would be hard to do.
They stay on the straight and narrow, God's will to pursue.
The staff at Ridgecrest is the best to be found
And I trust for many years they will be around.

Our pastor is young, but God-fearing and spirit led
And when I leave the service my soul has been fed.
The Pastor preaches, and of Jesus he is not ashamed.
From His Holy word, the message of God is proclaimed.

With humble spirit, singing of the choir and congregation,
I wait for the moving of the Spirit with great anticipation.
You can pray in the pew or you can kneel at the altar
We all need prayer and forgiveness, because we all falter.

With the feeling of guilt, I am weighted down.
At the altar, my spirit is lifted; forgiveness I have found.
An invitation is given and may be the last chance for some.
I pray, then weep for joy as one by one they come.

Sins have been confessed, souls saved, forgiveness received
And will spend an eternity in heaven because they believed.
Forgiven and renewed and though the scars of sin remain,
Into the world I go, with hope and a renewed spirit, again.

To hear the words of life, the scriptures explained so clearly,
I vow to treat others better and to love them more dearly.
For I serve a risen Savior, I know His words are true,
And for peace, and the joy of salvation, I pray you do too.

Yes, it is Sunday morning once more, it is that time of the week
When I go to church, God's blessings and forgiveness to seek.
At Ridgecrest Baptist Church, it is just another Sunday
Where I go to renew my faith to face another Monday.

RIDGECREST SERVICE

On Vaughn Road is Ridgecrest Baptist Church
Where on Sunday the scriptures we search.
We find and learn truths to live by,
To speak of salvation, we are not shy.

To spread the gospel, that's what we do.
Its God's commandment to me and you.
Point them to Jesus, His saving power,
Wait not — this may be their final hour.

We sing songs full of joy and praise
That will calm our souls and our spirits raise.
We welcome guests as well as friends
As on us the love of God descends.

Feel His presence, be moved by His spirit.
Follow His word, not only hear it.
Then you will have peace in your soul.
You will be complete and will be made whole.

Without Jesus and His love, all is lost,
There is no anchor when tempest tossed.
There is no direction, you rush to and fro.
There is no seed from which faith can grow.

The Soul Has Been Released

Love can conquer many things, but death is not one of them.
It is something we must think about, no matter how grim.
We all must die; it is something we all must face.
Of seeking riches and glory, we must give up the chase.

Though love abounds and care is taken, death will not wait.
No preparation can prevent this kind of heartache.
It is something expected, something we know will come,
And yet, it's hard to accept, we are devastated, we are numb.

When joy has gone out of the life, the gleam out of the eye,
We must await the change, prepare to say our goodbye.
Always been healthy, always been active, fun to be with,
"When you have your health, you have everything" is not a
    myth.

When one is in pain and has lost the will to live,
Been a good father, good husband, has nothing more to give,
Of how much they are loved, this could be the test.
To really love someone is to wish for them the best.
Are we selfish to want to keep them for another day?
Or should we pray for release — is it a price too high to pay?
Accept the sadness, release the loved one, embrace the grief,
Remember the joys of a life shared, no matter how brief.

It is at this time when it's the hardest to love,
To be able to rejoice as the spirit soars above.
The body in its coffin lies beneath the sod.
The soul has been released and takes its place with God.

Even with the loss, the living must keep going.
At harvest time, there's no reaping without the sowing.
Sow the seeds of love and give roses to the living,
Where joy can be shared as a result of the giving.

Poems of Family

This section was written far my family members: my sister Elizabeth; three brothers, J C., John, and Benny; and their eight sons, my nephews.

The Thompson Family Tree

The family tree starting with Mama and Daddy goes like this:
There first was Elizabeth, who ended up being our only Sis.
Elizabeth met Joe and soon they would marry.
It was not long before they produced Jimmy and Larry.
Jimmy married Kathy and they had a son.
Joseph completed this family and they were done.
Larry and Kim have two sons, Luke and Lane.
With three grandsons, Elizabeth and Joe's life was never the same.

Mama and Daddy's second child was J. C.
This started another limb on the family tree.
After the Air Force, he took Dorothy as his wife.
Sons Robert and Jack have brought great joy into their life.
Robert married Tracy — this started another limb —
Their children, Zack and Lauren became two more stems.
Jack and Mindel married and became part of the family tree
Though live and active, it produced no more limbs as you see.

If you are into genealogy and are planning our family tree,
From the trunk of Mama and Daddy, my limb stops with me.

John Wayne was the fourth child, the next to last.
He met and married Barbara and the die was cast.

Tracy married Curtis, John and Barbara's first son.
Of their children, Joshua was first and Tyler the second one.
The second son Russell married Wendy and from them, Alex
   came.
Andrew and Jonathon's mother and Alex's are not the same.
Russell's first wife, Julie, is their mother.
The five in this family are as close as any other.

Benny is the last limb of this family tree.
For children, Johnny and Jody, and daughter Michelle makes
   three.
Michelle was taken early, being with us only a few years.
She has been missed and remembered with many tears.
Benny's first wife, the mother of the children was Genell.
For some reason, that marriage was destined to fail.
For Benny, the mantle of singleness, he wanted to shed,
And for this reason and love, Sherrie and he were wed.

Johnny and Cindy are one of two branches off Benny's limb.
Daughter Courtney and son Justine are their two stems.
Jody and Tina make up branch number two.
They are the only family with two daughters, it's true.
The two smaller branches are Brooke and Emily.
For now, this completes the Thompson family tree.

Family

There are five siblings in our family,
One girl, four boys, besides Mama and Daddy.
There is Elizabeth, J. C., John, Benny and me.
That means I have one sister and brothers, three.

Daddy died when I was thirteen in nineteen-fifty.
He was a hard worker and very thrifty.
He had to be, for we were poor and had little money.
We were always happy and his disposition was sunny.

When he died, he had been working at the mill.
At that time, it was not clean — the danger was real —
Brown lung and carcinogens we knew little about.
Then he got sick, couldn't work, and we had to do without.

Thanks to a garden, canned food, and hunting skills,
We always seemed to have food and ate to our fill.
Mom worked hard to keep us all fed,
To keep us warm and a roof over our head.

After school, we became hunters, J. C. and I.
We got food for the table, anything we didn't have to buy.
We hunted squirrels, rabbits and anything else we could eat.
With a hot biscuit, Mama's fried squirrel was hard to beat.

We all helped out, and looked after one another.
We picked berries and figs, which were canned by our mother.
In those old glass jars, she put up peas, beans and corn,
And mended our shirts and pants when they were torn.

We may have been poor but we didn't know it,
And even if we did, we worked hard to not show it.
Mama kept us clean and saw that we looked good.
We took care of our clothes, did what we could.

Most times we were happy and got along well,
When we were not, no one could tell,
For we stuck together through thick and thin,
They are not only your family, but also your best friend.

ELIZABETH AND JOE

Elizabeth married into the Taylor clan
And found in Joe a successful man.
They were made for each other, or so it would seem.
Working together they have made a good team.

There are three grandsons, Jimmy one and Larry two,
With a family like this there is always something to do.
Jimmy is the older of their two boys,
And with the grandsons, there are lots of toys.

Elizabeth worked at the mill until a few years ago.
This does not mean she has stopped working, though.
She cooks every day for family and friends,
And for anyone else who just may drop in.

At Elizabeth's and Joe's, we have Christmas dinner.
With all the food there, we don't get any thinner.
She will have cakes and pies and custards, too.
You can't eat just one, that just won't do.

She helped support the family before she wed.
We had only Dad's Social Security to keep us fed.
I will always be grateful for all she did,
For she made a great difference in the life of this kid.

Jimmy and Kathy

Jimmy is Elizabeth and Joe's oldest son,
But they have two so he is not the only one.
He has a younger brother called Larry,
But this is about Jimmy, so on the younger let's not tarry.

After Jimmy got his degree, he took Kathy as his wife.
Together they have been successful and have a good life.
It wasn't long after marriage that Joseph came to be,
And with that, the family became three.

Jimmy is in Corrections and works for the State,
Kathy is a teacher and is his helpmate.
The school where Kathy teaches is quiet near,
Listen closely and the children you will hear.

Joseph attends this school but is not in her class,
When he is in the hall, he also needs a pass.
Jimmy's work is different; he keeps the prisoners in.
I wouldn't like his job — everyday going to "the pen."

They are successful in their chosen occupation.
They need perseverance as well as dedication.
With their hard work, retirement will be good
And maybe it will be as great as they hoped it would.

LARRY AND KIM

Larry is the youngest son of Elizabeth and Joe.
He has six chicken houses all in a row.
Before he had the chickens he married Kim.
He takes care of her and she takes care of him.

To complete this family are their two boys,
So full of life and two sources of great joy.
They have their own talents and ways to make you smile.
With his own personality, each is a special child.

Kim is a pharmacist at the local Wal-Mart.
To get a degree in this, she had to be pretty smart.
With chickens, the farm, and her job, they have done quite
    well—
The big house, the truck, the car, by all these you can tell.

They enjoy the outdoors and both enjoy their work,
Being able to spend time with family is just one of the perks.
I am glad they are in the family, part of the clan
And I hope we will still get together as often as we can.

J. C. and Dorothy

J. C. and Dorothy were married while still young
And before long they were the parents of two sons.
There was Robert first and then came Jack;
After that there was no looking back.

They have a nice home and have made a good living
Even though from their resources they are always giving.
To the church, to the family or to anyone else,
They make the most of the hand they have been dealt.

They were always there with anything Mom needed
And never left 'til all the chores were completed.
When Mom was sick and needed clothes cleaned,
Dorothy always did the washing, or so it seemed.

Since they have been together — both Dorothy and J. C. —
Where one goes, the other one you will see.
But with Dorothy still working and J. C. at home,
They must be apart and sometimes you see one alone.

They are more in love now than at the beginning
Even though they are older and J. C.'s hair is thinning.
They go together and were meant for each other.
I am glad to call them my sister-in-law and brother.

Robert and Tracy

Robert looked around and Tracy he did catch.
From the very beginning, it was a good match.
In the job he has chosen, he has done very well
And seems to enjoy his work as far as I can tell.

Robert is in law enforcement, a very unlikely job.
I just cannot see him trying to control a mob.
They enjoy each other and their children, too.
Zack and Lauren are both doing well in school.

Tracy has a good job and is working on a degree.
She has ability, grit, and determination, I can see.
In an area of law, she enjoys her job, too.
They will be successful in whatever they choose to do.

They were in Montgomery but moved to Prattville,
And live in a big house at the top of the hill.
They commute to work but have a good life
And it is a joy to call them nephew and wife.

JACK AND MINDELL

Jack and Mindell is a couple that is free.
They have nothing to tie them down, like me.
Though perfectly suited, I don't know how they met,
But I am almost sure, it was not on the Internet.

He gets you the picture and she makes you look great,
He with cable TV and she, with the hair on your pate.
She is good at what she does, and he is too.
Go to her for a hair cut, but he will come to you.

He likes to hunt and has killed many a deer.
Mindell has gone, but not as often, or so I hear.
Their abode is quite cozy; it's a doublewide.
It is in Opp at one-oh-six Terrie Drive.

They are a fine couple, this Mindell and Jack
And for family and friends, they do not lack.
They always seem to have a good time, I have found,
And for this reason it's joy to have them around.

Tyson, That's Me

Willie Tyson Thompson —known as "Tyson" — that's me,
Lived a full and happy life, being single and free.
My family consisted of me, one sister and three brothers,
And to complete the family, there was Daddy and our
Mother.

I attended Opp City Schools for twelve years
Where I had many friends among my peers.
We lived in town, I walked to school.
My third year, we moved and I rode the bus as a rule.

My freshman year in the band, I played a baritone,
Taught by our band director, Mrs. Mildred Carbone.
I switched to playing bass horn in my senior year,
Which played a major role in how I got to here.

My senior year I played in the All State Band
And it turned out better than what I had planned.
Because of this, I got a music scholarship to Southwest.
I could play the bass horn, but I surely wasn't the best.

Southwest was in Mississippi, a long way from home.
I had a friend who went with me so I was not alone.
With a music scholarship, I worked at a service station, too.
If I was going to college there was nothing else to do.

It was not hard work but it took up the weekend.
Sunday mornings were free, so church I did attend.
My second year, lab assistant was an added chore.
That left not much time to do anything more.

There was a bears' cage, with tennis courts just beyond.
Across the road in front of the dorm was a big pond.
I remember Junior College as a time of great fun.
We would play in the pond when our work was done.

Next, I attended Troy State Teachers' College
Where more science and math increased my knowledge.
In order to get my degree and become a better teacher,
I graduated and became an educated creature.

With my degree, off to Montgomery I went to teach.
It was chemistry and biology; physics was out of my reach.
For seventeen years I taught, wondering where the time went,
And finally ended up chairman of the Science Department.

After seventeen years, I took a job with the State.
It was a good job and was the best move I could make.
For two years I was in drug education before the change came.
Federal Programs was a regulatory program, it just was not the
      same.

My two programs —Title Two and Title Six —were new.
I was there for nineteen years, as coordinator for the last two.
With the incentive the Governor gave, I decided to get out.
Retirement is great and I am much happier, without a doubt.

The life of a retired state employee is not bad.
I enjoy it with more free time than I have ever had.
To read, write, travel or visit family, whatever I care to.
When you have forty years in your retirement, so can you.

JOHN AND BARBARA

For John and Barbara, this poem I pen —
Two of my favorite people of all my kin.
They have been together a very long time;
The marriage they have is one of a kind.

They have sons, daughters-in-law, and grandsons, too.
John and Barbara are proud of them whatever they do.
They get together often, especially on holidays,
When together they show their love in so many ways.

Tracy and Wendy are always friendly and warm,
Lively conversation with joyful laughter is the norm.
They are always ready with a hug and a smile,
They are open and easy to talk with — it is just their style.

Barbara works at the Mill and John, for the State.
Both are looking to retire before it's too late.
Then they can go anywhere and do as they please,
Visit their friends, their kin and other families.

They are part of the Thompson family, the kin, the clan.
They stick together, with the family they stand.
I am glad they are part of my family and that they care.
They are a loving couple and a permanent pair.

CURTIS AND TRACY

Curtis is the oldest boy of Barbara and John.
Like the other brothers and sister, they have two sons, not one.
Curtis met Tracy and soon wedding rings they wore,
Not long after, the family of two had become a family of four.

Their two sons are theirs you can tell.
They are a joy to be around and lively as well.
Joshua is the older and Tyler the younger,
They once were very small but not any longer.

Both Curtis and Tracy work at the mill,
They have good jobs and I trust always will.
A job is necessary for a successful life,
And nothing is more helpful than a supporting wife.

In their family of two sons, a father and mother,
You can tell from their actions, they love one another.
They are part of my family and I am part of theirs,
We stick together in all our troubles and cares.

RUSSELL AND WENDY

Russell is the only nephew with three sons,
But for Wendy, his wife, she has only one.
Before they were married, Russell had two.
They are now one family, nothing else would do.

It was Andrew and Jonathon, and now it's Alex, too,
All three are boys through and through.
They enjoy life and have a good time,
By their grades, you know they have good minds.

Andrew and Jonathon will work to make the good grades,
For this, good money they will be paid.
This will make it easier for them to enjoy life,
Especially when they have children and a wife.

And then there is Alex who will soon be in school
Where he will learn to read, write and the golden rule.
This little family is part of the Thompson family too.
They are happy and warm and I am glad it's true.

BENNY AND SHERRIE

Benny was a single father when he met Sherrie.
When he got to know her, he said, "Why tarry?"
And so married, they began a new life,
With Benny, his two sons and she as his new wife.

Benny worked at Dorsey Trailers for many years
And was a good worker, if one can believe what one hears.
He now works around the house and out in the yard.
Now he can forget about punching that time card.

Sherrie is still employed and still on the clock,
Waiting until she can sit on the porch and rock.
'When they can spend their hard-earned money
On the grand kids, who are bright and funny.

Johnny and Jody have two children of their own,
Jody, two girls, and Johnny, a girl and a son.
All four grandchildren are funny and bright.
And their parents are determined to bring them up right.

JOHNNY AND CINDY

Johnny met Cindy and soon they were wed.
It was love at first sight or so it has been said.
He worked at Dorsey, she at Wal-Mart,
You can tell by looking, she stole his heart.

They have two children, a girl and a boy,
Justine and Courtney are great sources of joy.
They are both in school and doing quiet well,
From their grades, you can tell.

Johnny has had several jobs and Cindy, too,
With what they have, they seem to make do.
It cannot be easy with a family of four
But they use what they have until they can get more.

They enjoy life and seem to have a good time,
At least it appears that way at Christmas time.
It is a sweet family, with a lot of love
And I pray there will always be blessings from above.

JODY AND TINA

Tina works at home and Jody at the Mill.
By looking at them you know their love is real.
She keeps the house, he works for pay,
And they are together at the end of the day.

Jody paints cars for extra money,
To call it extra seems funny.
It takes it all for a family of four
And sometimes there is need for even more.

Tina stays home to clean and cook
For their two girls, Emily and Brooke.
Emily and Brooke, each a very sweet child,
A little older and they will drive the boys wild.

They are in my prayers for happiness and health,
For there are different ways to measure wealth.
To be rich, to love and be loved is all you need
And for this family, they are rich indeed.

BETTY AND MARY

Betty and Mary are two family friends.
At my Christmas supper, they are asked to attend.
Betty is Mindell's mother, Mary, her aunt,
When asked to help, neither ever says, "I can't."

They mean a lot to the family, and to Dorothy and J. C.
And over the years, they have come to mean a lot to me.
They know the family of the Thompson clan,
And when we have pictures made, with us they stand.

They live a life of leisure, having plenty of time
To read, clean house or take a nap if they've a mind.
They can relax, rest and just take it easy,
No need to fuss, rush about, or get in a tizzy.

Life is too short to get upset and worry
Or fill you are behind and must get in a hurry.
They take it easy, live at a slower pace,
They worked hard to get out of the rat race.

Betty and Mary, I am glad to have them around,
Two more friendly people are not to be found.
These two women I like, Betty and Mary, too.
I'm glad they are part of our family, aren't you?

About the Author

W. Tyson Thompson was born and reared in Opp, Alabama. He attended Southwest Mississippi Junior College in Summit, Mississippi, on a music scholarship before transferring to Troy State Teachers College, now called Troy State University. While at Troy State he earned a Bachelor's Degree in Science. He did graduate work at Birmingham-Southern College, Birmingham, Alabama, and the University of Mississippi, in Oxford, Mississippi, where he earned a Master's Degree in Combined Sciences. Thompson taught chemistry and biology at Sidney Lanier High School in Montgomery, Alabama, for seventeen years before taking a position with the Alabama State Department of Education. He was with the Drug Education Program for three years before transferring to the Federal Programs Section where he spent the last nineteen years; the last two years in the SDE, he was Coordinator of Title II and Title VI. Thompson retired in September of 1998.

www.ingramcontent.com/pod-product-compliance
Lightning Source LLC
Chambersburg PA
CBHW031443120626
46545CB00006B/2527